AF820698

<u>CASE DISMISSED: How to Win Your Retail Fraud Case</u>

Jonathan A. Paul, Esq.

ISBN:

DEDICATION

To Mom
Who always told me to reach for the stars, because anything is possible

<u>MICHIGAN RETAIL FRAUD 101</u>

If you've been charged with Michigan Retail Fraud this doesn't make you a criminal or a bad person. I see clients on a daily basis who have have never been arrested in their life, or have a relapse, because of an addiction to stealing, which they thought was in the past. It's quite common that a good person will get themselves in a bad situation, which results in being charged with a Michigan Retail Fraud. Once charged, we can't go back in time and make it go away, but what we can do, is be proactive from day one and WIN.

The title of this book CASE DISMISSED: How to Win Your Retail Fraud Case is my goal in every case I agree to take on with a client. No matter how guilty you may be, or what situation you're in, this will be the first goal that we discuss. While every case is different, I don't recall a single retail fraud case, which I was not able to set my client up for a dismissal of charges.

If you're reading this book, you or someone you care about is likely charge with the serious offense of retail fraud. I encourage you to take your time with this book, and learn as much as possible about both the consequences, but also the opportunities that may be available if the charged person is willing to put the necessary work in from day one.

The crime of retail fraud is by far the most common offense for a first offender, and a crime that tends to be repeated. It's disheartening to sit across from a person who can't explain why they committed the crime or just can't stop their impulses, and they wish could go back in time and not make the same mistake.

I work with people from all different walks of life; I've worked with doctors, nurses, lawyers, airline pilots, police officers, fireman government workers, union members, stay-at-home parents, teachers, students, and just about every other profession in Michigan.

A conviction for retail fraud could be extremely damaging for keeping or getting a new job. This is where I come into play; I help clients every single day who are charged with this life altering offense. Retail fraud in Michigan is a crime of theft, fraud and dishonesty, and it will likely impact your current job, and all future employment.

I help clients take control of their case from day one by being proactive, and putting the incident in the past, and moving forward in a positive direction, which will help them make better choices going forward.

The crime of Retail Fraud in Michigan is something that is possible to have dismissed or reduced if the client is willing to put in the hard work upfront, and earn this incredible result. My clients from day one set a goal of keeping this incident off of their criminal record.

When a client first calls me, I will want to know about their past, and if they have a prior criminal record. From there, I will want to know where this happened and who was involved. We begin the fact gathering process together, and start to put together our comprehensive game plan. I call this the information gathering stage.

From there, we will order all of the police reports and evidence in the case. We may be able to track down video and audio, and if necessary will get a private investigator involved to build your various defenses. As a former prosecutor, I begin working with the prosecuting attorney on the case to explore all of your options.

This will be a two part approach, and when I use the term WIN, this means both inside and outside the courtroom. WINNING is about getting your case dismissed or reduced, and keeping retail fraud off your record, but it is also learning more about yourself, and how you found yourself charged with this crime. It's my goal as your attorney to put the tools in place to help guide you in future decisions; I never want you have to represent you again, but because we're going to fix this the first time. WINNING is about the present and the future. Here are the two ways we approach cases:

Retail Fraud Litigation - AKA Fighting the Charges

The first approach is to work to defeat your case either by a dismissal or a not guilty verdict at trial. This means your constitutional rights were in some way violated, which requires evidence of the crime to be dismissed, or you simply have a defense that you didn't steal, and we decide to take your case to trial where the prosecution must proof beyond a reasonable doubt that you committed the offense.

Michigan Retail Fraud requires the prosecution to prove beyond a reasonable doubt that:

#1 - the defendant took some property that the store offered for sale

#2 - the defendant moved the property (Any movement is enough. It does not matter whether the defendant actually got the property past the cashier or out of the store)

#3 - the defendant intended to steal the property. Intended to steal means that the defendant intended to permanently take the property from the store without the store's consent.

#4 - this happened either inside the store or in the immediate area around the store, while the store was open to the public.

#5 - the property has some value

If the value of the property is below $200, it is Michigan Retail Fraud in Third Degree, which is a 93 day misdemeanor.

If the value of the property is between $200-$1,000, it is Michigan Retail Fraud in Second Degree, which is a one year misdemeanor.

If the value of the property is more than $1,000, it is Michigan Retail Fraud in the First Degree, which is a felony.

Retail Fraud Negotiation- AKA Working out a Plea Deal

The second approach is based on your performance on the proactive program, and your positive changes since the offense; it may be possible to resolve your case regardless of how guilty you are of the offense, with a dismissal or reduction of charges outcome.

When you're charged with Retail Fraud in Michigan, the prosecutor, judge, the police department and your community assume that you are a thief, who has stolen items in the past, and you will continue to do so going forward if you are not severely punished. The truth is, that many people who are charged with this crime simply had a moment of poor judgment and otherwise have never done this before, nor would they do so in the future.

Unfortunately there is no way to distinguish the people who deserve a second chance from the people who need to be punished, and learn a tough lesson in life with jail and a criminal record.

My clients are provided the tools and resources to demonstrate that they should be considered in the group of people who deserve another chance; a chance to walk away from their case without going to jail, and without having a criminal record for the rest of their life.

You will have options, and together as a team, we decide your best path for your case, and WIN your case.

WHY PEOPLE STEAL IN MICHIGAN

According to experts on the subject, the crime of shoplifting in Michigan can be broken into a few different categories. Each of these categories has its own personality traits and different reactions to being caught and charged.

About half of all retail fraud crimes in Michigan are committed by compulsive shoplifters. Just like an alcoholic, drug user, gambler or problem eater, the problem lies in personal issues going on in one's life usually associated with anger or depression.

The items this group tends to steal are inexpensive, without much value to the person stealing them, but they simply can't help themselves. It's like the alcoholic who drinks straight from a ten dollar bottle of cheap vodka. There's little enjoyment/taste or flavor from the experience, but they simply don't care. Many times these people actually steal for others or give to people less fortunate. Many of these people have good paying jobs, money and credit cards in their pocket, and could easily afford the items.

This type of shoplifter will usually act shameful and guilty to the loss prevention officer, often cry or beg to be let go, and will likely confess to the entire offense without much prodding. This type of shoplifter will usually make winning a retail fraud case quite difficult due to a full confession, which will satisfy the prosecutor's burden of needing to show intent to steal the items.

The next category recognized by experts are the professional shoplifter who makes a living off stealing from stores. This shoplifter is the opposite of the compulsive shoplifter in that they will often target high-end items or multiple items.

These shoplifters often have a lot of experience, and have researched techniques to steal from stores, often using special tools or techniques to evade being caught. This shoplifter does not show emotion, and will often not speak to the loss prevention officers or the police department. This type of shoplifter may try to leave the scene. If successful, this type of shoplifter will often attempt to sell the items on the internet or to others for money.

The next category is the shoplifter who steals due to need, and not luxury, greed or compulsion. This shoplifter will steal food, clothing or hygiene products for themselves or their family. Many times the high cost of a newborn baby will cause a family member to steal to provide for that baby such as expensive baby formula. This type of shoplifter will act sad and often admit to the reason for stealing the items.

The next category is the person who steals for the thrill/fun of it. Many people get a high off stealing from a store, but it is not a compulsion where they cannot help themselves. Often this type of stealing happens in young kids who simply want to be cool or show friends that they can do it. Often times this type of shoplifter will not say much to loss prevention or the police department.

The next category is the person who steals to maintain another habit. They are not addicted to shoplifting itself, but rather alcohol, drugs or gambling. Someone needs to get their fix and lacks the money to support it. They view shoplifting as a means to the money they need to support their habit and would rather risk the consequences than not be able to get their fix.

This category goes for high-end items with the possibility of a big return on their risk. This category can turn into the professional thief if they continue to steal to support their habit, but many times the idea of stealing is a last resort, and being caught stealing will hopefully lead to the person getting help for their real habit.

The final category is the person who simply doesn't mean to steal the item(s). Many parents with children with them, elderly people, people on medication or suffering from memory issues will leave a store without paying for an item. This person lacks the intent, and are not actually guilty of anything. The issue remains, the prosecutor will still prosecute you, and force you to show your innocence at a trial.

WHO STEALS THE MOST IN MICHIGAN?

According to statistics published by the State of Michigan, it is quite interesting to review the different breakdowns.

What months have the highest rate of theft crimes?

For theft crimes in Michigan, the summer tends to be the most popular with July at 15,221, August with 14,877 and June with 13.814. The months with the least amount of theft crimes are December, January and February.

Comment: Most would think the holiday seasons would be the highest, but due to extra security presence, it appears that people are concerned about being caught.

What days of the week have the most theft crimes?

It appears that Monday and Friday are the most popular days for theft crimes in Michigan with 22,819 on Monday and 22,971 on Friday. Sunday is by far the day with the least amount of offenses at 17,222.

Comment: It would seem like the weekend would be the most popular day, but people shop with others, including children on the weekends, and likely tend to steal when they are by themselves during the week.

What was the financial impact of theft in Michigan?

Total property loss values for all property crimes was $671,467,809. For larcenies, this equates to 46 percent of the state value.

What are the most common ages for people charged with retail fraud?

Juveniles (16 years and under) accounted for 2,271 offenses, while 25-29 was the most frequent age group at 2,582, followed by 30-34 at 2,000. After that 35-39 was 1,360 offenses, 40-44 at 1,236, 45-49 at 1088, 50-54 at 930, 55-59 at 546 and 60 and older at 428

Comment: Clearly retail fraud does not escape any age category, as I have personally represented clients as young at 14, and as old as 77 years old.

What are the most common races for people charged with retail fraud?

The most common race for retail fraud in Michigan was Caucasian with 15,793 cases; the next was African American with 9,345 cases then unknown was 949 cases, Asian with 125 cases and American Indian with 126 cases.

Who gets charged more, men or women?

The stats show men were charged 14,394 times with retail fraud in Michigan and 11,944 women are charged with the offense.

Comment: Over the years, I've represented about double the women than man, which makes this an interesting statistic.

CONSEQUENCES

When a potential client contacts me, they ask what the possible consequences could be if they are convicted of retail fraud. I tell them there are criminal consequences at the courthouse then additional consequences that will impact their daily life, including their career. In order to WIN your case, both of these factors must be addressed from day one.

First off, depending upon what you level of retail fraud you're charged with, jail time could be 93 days or one year, and if it's a felony, the maximum is five years in prison. In additional to jail and prison time, there is the possibility of up to 24 months probation for a misdemeanor and 60 months for a felony.

There are mandatory fines and costs associated with each charge, possible alcohol and drug testing, community service, inpatient or outpatient treatment, education, attendance at support group meetings, ban from leaving the State of Michigan and a host of other probation sanctions. Most damaging is having a criminal conviction on your record. A criminal record of theft, fraud and dishonesty. Much of this can be avoided by taking action from day one, and approaching your case with a WINNING attitude.

If you're applying for a job, loan, college, grad school, professional license military service or even filling out a chaperone form for your kid's class trip, you will have to answer YES to having a criminal record/being convicted of a crime, and more specifically a crime of theft and dishonesty. It's doubtful you will ever be trusted to handle money or sensitive information again.

I work with a number of clients with different jobs and professions. There are specific types of jobs where a retail fraud conviction could cost you your license such as a nurse, doctor, pharmacist, attorney, teacher airline pilot, accountant, financial planner etc. There are about 500 different jobs/careers in my experience, which can be lost due to this sort of conviction.

There are also additional consequences for CPL holders, licensed drivers, people on probation or parole, people going through custody of divorce proceedings and clients who are not U.S. citizens.

It's important to make your attorney aware of every single license, "situation" and current or future career goals you may have. Many clients don't think that a concealed weapon permit would impacted by a retail fraud conviction, then suddenly get a letter in the mail suspending their license for a year. Many people rely on a CPL for their safety and job, and a suspension puts that person in great personal and financial danger.

Each case has it's own facts and circumstances. Depending upon the prosecutor and the judge, we will discuss possible options for your case. Many retail fraud cases are facts that are stacked against the client.

Many clients are caught red-handed and/or make full admissions to the offense, and make a trial a non-viable option. Some clients must concede that they simply made a choice that was illegal and has consequences.

Fortunately for the clients that I represent, they follow my proactive program, and put themselves in a position to have their retail fraud charges dismissed or reduced. It's possible to WIN even when all the facts are against you, because you control the outcome by taking action.

In the end, my client's main goal is to avoid a retail fraud conviction, and this goal can be accomplished a number of ways either with a trial or a reduction or dismissal. All clients go on my proactive plan, which not only helps the case at the courthouse, but also helps my clients outside the courtroom stay out of trouble, learn from their situation and move forward in a positive direction for their family and career.

HOW TO WIN YOUR CASE

When a potential client contacts me, I inform them that my services are very exclusive, and I turn down more clients than I agree to represent. The reason I do this, is because each retail fraud case requires a great deal of my attention in order to put my client in the best position possible to WIN THE CASE.

Most clients who contact me tell me their #1 goal is to keep the charge of retail fraud off of their record, because they fear losing a job, being denied a license, the stigma of being a criminal, and many other reasons. All of these reasons are valid, and depending upon one's profession, there are extra precautions needed, such as a health care professional or a teacher. Depending upon your career, we will discuss implications of different outcomes, and options to resolve your case.

Another goal that a client may have is avoiding jail time. I tell clients that as a first time offender for retail fraud, or even a second offender, generally jail time is not likely to happen. This does not mean it could not happen, but based on my experience with the particular court, prosecutor and judge, I should be able to tell you immediately if jail is a real possibility or a long shot.

Sometimes we speak to the the judge ahead of time and request a COBBS agreement, meaning the judge promises not to send you to jail in exchange for the plea deal. When you know the outcome, you WIN. You can only WIN if you have clear goals to accomplish, and a plan to achieve those goals.

Many clients who contact me simply tell me they want the CASE DROPPED. This is simply not going to happen without going to court at least one time. The police and prosecutor gathering enough information about your case in order to charge you. It is not their job to determine if you're guilty or not - that is the purpose of going to court and hiring your own attorney.

Many innocent people are charged with retail fraud, because the loss prevention officer, store employees and the police are not able to read your mind. Retail fraud requires INTENT TO STEAL, and they may watch you, and the perception is well you meant to steal, why else would you try to leave the store with unpaid items? You can yell and scream all you want that you didn't mean to do it, but that is not going to get you anywhere with them. It will also not get you anywhere once charged. If you want to proceed on that, then it will require a trial, and likely your testimony on the witness stand.

A trial by judge or jury is one way to pursue your goals of no criminal record and avoiding jail. It is also a risky option, but sometimes the only option for someone who simply had no intent on stealing the items they are being accused of stealing. If this applies to your case, a comprehensive trial plan and a not guilty verdict at trial is the way to WIN THE CASE. If you're found guilty at trial then you have the charge on your record, and you could be sent to jail.

Rolling the dice, and not controlling the situation is not a WINNING approach. If we can accomplish our goals with no risk, then it may be the better option for your case. If those options are not on the table, then it's time to go to trial, and make the best out of a limited situation. I've yet to run into a case where I could not reach a WINNING outcome.

Many people do not realize that there are far riskier ways to WIN THE CASE. One option may be to pursue a diversion with the prosecutor or judge; an agreement of some sort of reduction or dismissal that does not challenge your guilt or innocence, but rather considers the facts of the case along with your background, career, lack of criminal record, and what you had done since being charged. The last part is by far the key to WIN YOUR CASE. My comprehensive proactive defense for retail fraud is the key to reaching my client's goals.

If you simply did not have the intent to steal, and would never even think to steal, those words alone are not enough to get your case dismissed. A prosecutor and judge don't care about words and promises, they care about real actions. If I agree to take on a client's case, they begin my proactive program one day one, and begin putting real actions into place, which demonstrate to a judge or prosecutor who they really are; a productive, law-abiding person who understands the situation before them, and the situation alone is enough to learn from it, and make sure they are never in that situation again.

There are many ways to WIN THE CASE when charged with retail fraud. It depends on your goals and how you define a win. My client's set realistic goals and a plan is put into place on how to reach those goals. Over the course of the case, with my guidance and counseling, my client works on my program, and the end result is a WIN.

It's extremely important to pick the right attorney who fits your personality. I am extremely demanding of my clients, because I expect them to work hard, and earn a great result. I can't do the hard work for them; I can provide the ingredients, but the client has to cook their own meal. My philosophy of WINNING may mean that I am tougher on my client than the judge and prosecutor will be. If the client can impress me while on my demanding program, going to court will be easy enough.

It's our goal to create the exact outcome that we want, and simply convince the judge and prosecutor to agree, and adopt our proposal. When you decide the outcome of your case, that is a WINNING result.

BEING PROACTIVE

Retail fraud cases in Michigan have four outcomes. Your case could be dismissed due to suppression of evidence or unavailability of a witness, you may enter into a negotiated plea agreement to a reduced charge with a sentencing agreement, which keeps you out of jail, you may go to trial and be found not guilty or you go to trial and you're found guilty.

So how do I get you the best outcome for your Michigan Retail Fraud case? How do you WIN your case? As a former New York City and Michigan prosecutor I know both sides of this system, and I know what gets results.

My method of criminal defense is unique, because my clients take a proactive approach rather than sitting back and simply hoping for things to go well. This approach has worked in courts all around Michigan and for various criminal charges. I've yet to find a case where my program has not resulted in some sort of eventual dismissal.

My approach has sometimes resulted in better bond conditions, less or no alcohol/drug testing, dismissal of charges, avoiding jail, shorter probation terms, lower fines and costs and a number of other benefits. My clients get great satisfaction knowing that they can have a positive influence on their case both inside and outside the courtroom.

When you're charged with retail fraud in Michigan you're considered a criminal by the court, prosecutor and police department. Your case and file have no face, history, background or information other than the crime you're alleged to have committed. No wonder most judges and prosecutors only think of you as a criminal who deserves to be punished. I know that's not the case, but we need to convince them of the same thing. You WIN your case when you change the perception of who you are with the judge and prosecutor.

This is where my game plan takes over, and begins to turn this vicious cycle around. On my plan, we create positive currency to counteract all the negative vibes around your case. Do good honest people make mistakes? You bet. Does a judge or prosecutor think you're actually a good person who deserves a second chance? Right now - NO! .... you don't get the benefit of the doubt by simply showing up in court.

Even if your attorney says how wonderful you are, those words are cheap, because any good attorney is going to speak well of his/her client. A court and prosecutor want real action! This is what we do as a team. We develop a specific game plan tailored to your case and your background in order to present you as the good and honest person that you are - a good person who made a mistake or had a lapse in judgment.

Without doing this a judge may think you need to be taught a lesson by going to jail, or the judge can't trust you not to drink or do drugs, and wants to test you twice a day on your own dime. Wouldn't it just be easier to start a program before even going to court, do well on it, and ask a judge to just continue allowing you to do that rather than what he had in mind for you?

It's like creating your own punishment as a kid and having your parents accept it rather than them coming up with their own terms. You WIN when you decide the outcome.

By being proactive outside of the courtroom, it helps when you get in the courtroom. I provide the tools to accomplish your goals.

What if I'm innocent and don't think I should have to do anything?

Despite your constitutional right to be innocent until proven guilty, a court is still going to give you bond conditions, and can keep you in jail during your case. Just being charged with a crime allows the court to have total control over your life until your case is concluded. My plan puts all clients in a better position during their case, allowing the opportunity for my favorable bond conditions, because we're taking control of the situation for the judge.

Doesn't it just sound better, and makes you feel a little better if we can tell a judge you're attending retail fraud support group meetings voluntarily and doing community service rather than a judge yelling and screaming and telling you that you need to go?

Wouldn't be a good thing to take an education course on retail fraud, and tell the judge that you've already started learning how to prevent this behavior going forward? What about going to a counselor to discuss possible underlying issues in your life that lead to this isolated moment in time?

My clients go to court with answers to every question and concern that a judge and prosecutor may have about you. We anticipate resistance and go above and beyond to put ourselves in the very best position to create options for your case.

Most clients feel better about themselves and going to court when they are already being proactive about their case. It's the difference between studying for an exam and being confident versus just showing up and hoping something good happens. When you're prepared, you WIN.

During this proactive approach, we're also exploring every single defense to your case as a team. If the case can be defeated or won at trial, that is what we do. I've been a prosecutor in New York City and here in Michigan, if trial is your best option, we will go ahead and go down that path.

If we decide as a team that the cons outweigh the pros in pursuing that approach then our proactive approach is already in place, and your case is in a better position to be reduced, dismissed or some other favorable outcome, which may not have been possible without being proactive from the very beginning. A judge and prosecutor in my experience are going to look a lot more favorably on giving a client the benefit of the doubt if they are already doing things during their case.

How can you apply to be one of my clients?

No that's not a typo, potential clients must apply for my legal services. My services are in high demand, and I cannot represent every person that contacts me. By reading this book, you are already on the path to demonstrating a true motivation to follow my program, and reap the benefits.

I have to turn down around half of all potential clients that call or email me, for Retail Fraud cases in Michigan, because I'm either fully booked with my current clients or your case may not be the best fit for my law firm.

I carefully select clients who are committed to following my game plan, and want to better themselves going forward. If you simply want to show up and hope for the best, I can give you the name of another attorney who will take your money. If you want to WIN inside and outside the courtroom, I will help you.

When you contact me, I'll want to know what degree of Retail Fraud that you're charged with, where it happened and some background information on yourself. I want to know your goals and whether or not this is your first contact with the law. I use a basketball analogy to describe my approach.

We call a timeout, regroup and put forth a well thought out game plan, which results in an efficient and successful score on the offensive end. We don't sit back on our heels and play defense hoping not to lose. We work with the strengths of your case, and spin the negatives into positives.

As you read this, you're worried about going to jail, having a criminal record, losing a driver's license, and possibly losing a job, student loans, being kicked out of school or even being deported from this country.

Let me take that weight off your shoulders by explaining to you my method for defending your particular case. I promise that you'll feel better after speaking to me about your case and your goals. You will have a game plan in place, and will be actively involved in influencing the outcome of your case.

The average client feels isolated and helpless when charged with a crime; my clients are involved and actively doing things every day to improve their position and their future.

MICHIGAN CIRCUIT COURTS

In Michigan, the Circuit Court is the trial court with the broadest powers in Michigan. In general, the Circuit Court handles all civil cases with claims of more than $25,000 and all felony criminal cases (cases where the accused, if found guilty, could be sent to prison).

The family division of Circuit Court handles all cases regarding divorce, paternity, adoptions, personal protection actions, emancipation of minors, treatment and testing of infectious disease, safe delivery of newborns, name changes, juvenile offenses and delinquency, juvenile guardianship, and child abuse and neglect.

In addition, the Circuit Court hears cases appealed from the other trial courts or from administrative agencies. The friend of the court office is part of the family division of the Circuit Court and handles domestic relations cases where minor children are involved.

There are 57 Circuit Courts in Michigan. Circuit Court judges are elected for six-year terms. For retail fraud cases, if you are charged with a felony, your case will begin at the district court level for preliminary examination then proceed to the circuit court level for further proceedings such as a trial.

Here are the circuit courts, which I visit most often for retail fraud cases, and the different judges at this level of the criminal justice system. These listings are updated as of the publishing of this book. There may have been changes to some of this information after the publishing of this book.

6th Circuit Court - Oakland
Courthouse Tower
1200 N. Telegraph Rd.
Pontiac, MI 48341
(248) 858-0345

Honorable Nanci J. Grant, Chief Judge
Honorable James M. Alexander, Circuit Judge
Honorable Martha Anderson, Circuit Judge
Honorable Leo Bowman, Circuit Judge
Honorable Mary Ellen Brennan, Circuit Judge
Honorable Rae Lee Chabot, Circuit Judge
Honorable Lisa Ortlieb Gorcyca, Circuit Judge
Honorable Shalina D. Kumar, Circuit Judge
Honorable Denise Langford-Morris, Circuit Judge
Honorable Lisa Langton, Circuit Judge
Honorable Cheryl A. Matthews, Circuit Judge
Honorable Karen D. McDonald, Circuit Judge
Honorable Phyllis C. McMillen, Circuit Judge
Honorable Colleen A. O'Brien, Circuit Judge

Honorable Daniel Patrick O'Brien, Circuit Judge
Honorable Wendy Lynn Potts, Circuit Judge
Honorable Michael D. Warren, Jr., Circuit Judge
Honorable Joan E. Young, Circuit Judge

3rd Circuit Court - Frank Murphy Hall of Justice - Wayne

Frank Murphy Hall of Justice
1441 St. Antoine St.
Detroit, MI 48226
(313) 224-5261

Honorable Robert J. Colombo, Jr., Chief Judge
Honorable David J. Allen, Circuit Judge
Honorable Annette J. Berry, Circuit Judge
Honorable Gregory D. Bill, Circuit Judge
Honorable Ulysses W. Boykin, Circuit Judge
Honorable Karen Y. Braxton, Circuit Judge
Honorable Margie R. Braxton, Circuit Judge
Honorable Megan Maher Brennan, Circuit Judge
Honorable James A. Callahan, Circuit Judge
Honorable Thomas Cameron, Circuit Judge
Honorable Jerome C. Cavanagh, Circuit Judge
Honorable Eric William Cholack, Circuit Judge
Honorable James R. Chylinski, Circuit Judge
Honorable Kevin J. Cox, Circuit Judge
Honorable Daphne Means Curtis, Circuit Judge
Honorable Christopher D. Dingell, Circuit Judge
Honorable Charlene M. Elder, Circuit Judge
Honorable Vonda R. Evans, Circuit Judge
Honorable Edward Ewell, Jr., Circuit Judge
Honorable Patricia Susan Fresard, Circuit Judge
Honorable Sheila Ann Gibson, Circuit Judge
Honorable John H. Gillis, Jr., Circuit Judge
Honorable Alexis Glendening, Circuit Judge
Honorable David Alan Groner, Circuit Judge
Honorable Richard B. Halloran, Circuit Judge
Honorable Cynthia Gray Hathaway, Circuit Judge
Honorable Dana Margaret Hathaway, Circuit Judge
Honorable Daniel Arthur Hathaway, Circuit Judge
Honorable Michael M. Hathaway, Circuit Judge

Honorable Charles S. Hegarty, Circuit Judge
Honorable Catherine Heise, Circuit Judge
Honorable Susan L. Hubbard, Circuit Judge
Honorable Muriel D. Hughes, Circuit Judge
Honorable Edward Joseph, Circuit Judge
Honorable Connie Marie Kelley, Circuit Judge
Honorable Timothy Michael Kenny, Circuit Judge
Honorable Qiana D. Lillard, Circuit Judge
Honorable Kathleen I. Macdonald, Circuit Judge
Honorable Kathleen M. McCarthy, Circuit Judge
Honorable Bruce U. Morrow, Circuit Judge
Honorable John A. Murphy, Circuit Judge
Honorable Maria L. Oxholm, Circuit Judge
Honorable Lynne A. Pierce, Circuit Judge
Honorable Lita Masini Popke, Circuit Judge
Honorable Richard M. Skutt, Circuit Judge
Honorable Mark T. Slavens, Circuit Judge
Honorable Leslie Kim Smith, Circuit Judge
Honorable Virgil C. Smith, Circuit Judge
Honorable Martha M. Snow, Circuit Judge
Honorable Craig S. Strong, Circuit Judge
Honorable Brian R. Sullivan, Circuit Judge
Honorable Lawrence S. Talon, Circuit Judge
Honorable Deborah A. Thomas, Circuit Judge
Honorable Margaret M. Van Houten, Circuit Judge
Honorable Shannon N. Walker, Circuit Judge

<u>16th Circuit Court - Macomb</u>

Macomb County Court Building
40 N. Main
Mt. Clemens, MI 48043
(586) 469-5150

Honorable James M. Biernat, Jr., Chief Judge
Honorable Richard L. Caretti, Circuit Judge
Honorable Mary A. Chrzanowski, Circuit Judge
Honorable Diane M. Druzinski, Circuit Judge
Honorable Jennifer Faunce, Circuit Judge
Honorable James M. Maceroni, Circuit Judge
Honorable Edward A. Servitto, Jr., Circuit Judge
Honorable Mark S. Switalski, Circuit Judge

Honorable Matthew S. Switalski, Circuit Judge
Honorable Joseph Toia, Circuit Judge
Honorable Kathryn A. Viviano, Circuit Judge
Honorable Tracey A. Yokich, Circuit Judge

22nd Circuit Court - Washtenaw
PO Box 8645
Courthouse
101 E. Huron
Ann Arbor, MI 48107
(734) 222-3270

Honorable David S. Swartz, Chief Judge
Honorable Archie Cameron Brown, Circuit Judge
Honorable Patrick J. Conlin, Jr., Circuit Judge
Honorable Timothy P. Connors, Circuit Judge
Honorable Carol Anne Kuhnke, Circuit Judge

44th Circuit Court - Livingston
204 S. Highlander Way
Howell, MI 48843
(517) 546-8079
Honorable David Reader, Chief Judge
Honorable Michael P. Hatty, Circuit Judge

38th Circuit Court - Monroe
Monroe County Courthouse
106 E. First St.
Monroe, MI 48161
(734) 240-7020
Honorable Jack Vitale, Chief Judge
Honorable Mark S. Braunlich, Circuit Judge
Honorable Michael A. Weipert, Circuit Judge
Honorable Daniel White, Circuit Judge

39th Circuit Court - Lenawee
Rex B Martin Judicial Building
425 N. Main Street
Adrian, MI 49221
(517) 264-4597
Honorable Margaret Murray-Scholz Noe, Chief Judge

Honorable Anna Marie Anzalone, Circuit Judge

30th Circuit Court - Lansing - Ingham

PO Box 40771
Veterans Memorial Courthouse
313 W. Kalamazoo St.
Lansing, MI 48901
(517) 483-6500

Honorable Janelle A. Lawless, Chief Judge
Honorable Rosemarie E. Aquilina, Circuit Judge
Honorable Laura Baird, Circuit Judge
Honorable Clinton Canady, III, Circuit Judge
Honorable Joyce Draganchuk, Circuit Judge
Honorable James S. Jamo, Circuit Judge

4th Circuit Court - Jackson

312 S. Jackson St.
Jackson, MI 49201
(517) 788-4268

Honorable Thomas D. Wilson, Chief Judge
Honorable Susan E. Beebe, Circuit Judge
Honorable Richard N. LaFlamme, Circuit Judge
Honorable John G. McBain, Jr., Circuit Judge

7th Circuit Court - Genesee

Genesee County Courthouse
900 S. Saginaw St.
Flint, MI 48502
(810) 424-4355

Honorable Richard B. Yuille, Chief Judge
Honorable Duncan M. Beagle, Circuit Judge
Honorable Joseph J. Farah, Circuit Judge
Honorable Judith A. Fullerton, Circuit Judge
Honorable John A. Gadola, Circuit Judge
Honorable Archie L. Hayman, Circuit Judge

Honorable Geoffrey L. Neithercut, Circuit Judge
Honorable David J. Newblatt, Circuit Judge
Honorable Michael J. Theile, Circuit Judge

THE DISTRICT COURTS

Michigan District Courts are often called the people's court. More people have contact with the District Courts than any other court. The District Courts handles most traffic violations, all civil cases with claims up to $25,000, landlord-tenant matters, most traffic tickets, and all misdemeanor criminal cases (generally, cases where the accused, if found guilty, cannot be sentenced to more than one year in jail). In addition, small claims cases are heard by a division of the District Courts.

In Michigan, a few municipalities have chosen to retain a municipal court rather than create a District Courts. The municipal courts have limited powers and are located in Grosse Pointe, Grosse Pointe Farms, Grosse Pointe Park, and Grosse Point Shores/Grosse Pointe Woods.

There are approximately 100 District Courts in Michigan. District court judges are elected for six-year terms. Here are some of the district courts which I practice in the most. These listings are accurate as of the publishing of this week; things may change after the publishing of this book.

Washtenaw County

14A1 District Court - Ann Arbor - Washtenaw (D14A)

PO Box 8645
4133 Washtenaw Road
Ann Arbor, MI 48107
(734) 973-4545

Honorable Richard Conlin District Judge

14A2 District Court - Ypsilanti - Washtenaw (D14A)

415 W. Michigan Ave.
Ypsilanti, MI 48197
(734) 484-6690

Honorable Kirk W. Tabbey, District Judge

14A3 District Court - Chelsea - Washtenaw (D14A)

122 S. Main Street
Chelsea, MI 48118
(734) 475-8606

Honorable Richard E. Conlin, Chief Judge

14A4 District Court - Saline - Washtenaw (D14A)

1000 N. Maple Rd.
Saline, MI 48176
(734) 429-2504

Honorable Richard E. Conlin, Chief Judge
Honorable J. Cedric Simpson, District Judge
Honorable Kirk W. Tabbey, District Judge

14B District Court - Washtenaw (D14B)

Ypsilanti Township Civic Center
7200 S. Huron River Drive
Ypsilanti, MI 48197
(734) 483-1333

Honorable Charles Pope, Chief Judge

15th District Court - Washtenaw (D15)

PO Box 8650
Justice Center
301 E. Huron
Ann Arbor, MI 48104
(734) 794-6759

Honorable Elizabeth Pollard Hines, Chief Judge
Honorable Joseph F. Burke, District Judge
Honorable Christopher S. Easthope, District Judge

Genesee County

67th District Court - Flint - Genesee (D67-1)

630 S. Saginaw St.
Flint, MI 48502
(810) 257-3181
Honorable Richard B. Yuille, Chief Judge
Honorable David J. Goggins, District Judge

67th District Court - Flushing - Genesee (D67-1)

1415 Flushing Road
Flushing, MI 48433
(810) 659-5659
Honorable Richard B. Yuille, Chief Judge
Honorable David J. Goggins, District Judge

67th District Court - Burton - Genesee (D67-2)

4094 Manor Dr.
Burton, MI 48529
(810) 743-5600

Honorable Richard B. Yuille, Chief Judge
Honorable Mark W. Latchana, District Judge

67th District Court - Davison - Genesee (D67-2)

200 E. Flint St.
Davison, MI 48423
(810) 653-4126

Honorable Richard B. Yuille, Chief Judge
Honorable Jennifer J. Manley, District Judge

67th District Court - Mt. Morris - Genesee (D67-3)

11820 N. Saginaw St.
Mt. Morris, MI 48458

(810) 686-7140

Honorable Richard B. Yuille, Chief Judge
Honorable Vikki Bayeh Haley, District Judge

67th District Court - Fenton - Genesee (D67-4)

17100 Silver Parkway
Fenton, MI 48430
(810) 629-5318

Honorable Richard B. Yuille, Chief Judge
Honorable Mark C. McCabe, District Judge

67th District Court - Grand Blanc - Genesee (D67-4)

8173 S. Saginaw St.
Grand Blanc, MI 48439
(810) 694-2552

Honorable Richard B. Yuille, Chief Judge
Honorable Christopher Odette, District Judge

68th District Court - Genesee (D68)
630 S. Saginaw St.
Flint, MI 48502
(810) 766-8968

Honorable Richard B. Yuille, Chief Judge
Honorable Tracy L. Collier-Nix, District Judge
Honorable William H. Crawford, II, District Judge
Honorable Mary Catherine Dowd, District Judge
Honorable Herman Marable, Jr., District Judge
Honorable Nathaniel C. Perry, III, District Judge

Macomb County

38th District Court - Macomb (D38)

16101 Nine Mile Rd.
Eastpointe, MI 48021
(586) 445-5020

Honorable Carl F. Gerds, III, Chief Judge

39th District Court - Roseville - Macomb (D39~1)

29733 Gratiot Ave.
Roseville, MI 48066
(586) 773-2010

Honorable Catherine B. Steenland, Chief Judge
Honorable Joseph F. Boedeker, District Judge
Honorable Marco A. Santia, District Judge

39th District Court - Fraser - Macomb (D39~2)

PO Box 10
City Hall
33000 Garfield Rd.
Fraser, MI 48026
(586) 293-3137

Honorable Catherine B. Steenland, Chief Judge
Honorable Joseph F. Boedeker, District Judge
Honorable Marco A. Santia, District Judge

40th District Court - Macomb (D40)

27701 Jefferson Ave.
St. Clair Shores, MI 48081
(586) 445-5280

Honorable Joseph Craigen Oster, Chief Judge
Honorable Mark A. Fratarcangeli, District Judge

41A District Court - Sterling Heights - Macomb (D41A~1)

40111 Dodge Park Rd.
Sterling Heights, MI 48313
(586) 446-2500

Honorable Michael S. Maceroni, Chief Judge
Honorable Douglas P. Shepherd, District Judge
Honorable Stephen S. Sierawski, District Judge
Honorable Kimberley Anne Wiegand, District Judge

41A District Court - Shelby - Macomb (D41A~2)
51660 Van Dyke Ave.
Shelby Township, MI 48316
(586) 739-7325

Honorable Michael S. Maceroni, Chief Judge
Honorable Douglas P. Shepherd, District Judge
Honorable Stephen S. Sierawski, District Judge
Honorable Kimberley Anne Wiegand, District Judge

41B District Court - Macomb (D41B)

22380 Starks Dr.
Clinton Township, MI 48036
(586) 469-9300

Honorable Sebastian Lucido, Chief Judge
Honorable Linda Davis, District Judge
Honorable Carrie Lynn Fuca, District Judge

42nd District Court - Romeo - Macomb (D42-1)
PO Box 6
14713 33 Mile Rd.
Romeo, MI 48065
(586) 752-9679

Honorable James M. Biernat, Jr., Chief Judge
Honorable Denis R. LeDuc, District Judge

42nd District Court - New Baltimore - Macomb (D42-2)

35071 23 Mile Rd.
New Baltimore, MI 48047
(586) 725-9500

Honorable James M. Biernat, Jr., Chief Judge
Honorable William H. Hackel, III, District Judge

Livingston County

53rd District Court - Howell - Livingston (D53)

204 S. Highlander Way
Howell, MI 48843
(517) 548-1000

Honorable David Reader, Chief Judge
Honorable L. Suzanne Geddis, District Judge
Honorable Carol Sue Reader, District Judge

53rd District Court - Brighton - Livingston (D53)

224 N. First Street
Brighton, MI 48116
(810) 229-6615

Honorable David Reader, Chief Judge
Honorable Theresa M. Brennan, District Judge

54A District Court - Ingham (D54A)

City Hall, 6th Floor
124 W. Michigan Ave.
Lansing, MI 48933
(517) 483-4433

Honorable Louise Alderson, Chief Judge
Honorable Patrick F. Cherry, District Judge
Honorable Hugh B. Clarke, Jr., District Judge
Honorable Frank J. DeLuca, District Judge

Ingham County

54B District Court - Ingham (D54B)

101 Linden St.
East Lansing, MI 48823
(517) 351-7000
Honorable Andrea Andrews Larkin, Chief Judge
Honorable Richard D. Ball, District Judge

55th District Court - Ingham (D55)

700 Buhl Dr.
Mason, MI 48854
(517) 676-8400

Honorable Thomas P. Boyd, Chief Judge
Honorable Donald L. Allen, District Judge

Jackson County

12th District Court - Jackson (D12)

Jackson County Courthouse
312 S. Jackson St.
Jackson, MI 49201
(517) 788-4260

Honorable Michael J. Klaeren, Chief Judge
Honorable Joseph S. Filip, District Judge
Honorable Daniel A. Goostrey, District Judge
Honorable R. Darryl Mazur, District Judge

Wayne County

16th District Court - Wayne (D16)

32765 Five Mile Rd.
Livonia, MI 48154
(734) 466-2500

Honorable Sean P. Kavanagh, Chief Judge
Honorable Kathleen J. McCann, District Judge

17th District Court - Wayne (D17)

15111 Beech-Daly Rd.
Redford, MI 48239
(313) 387-2790

Honorable Karen Khalil, Chief Judge
Honorable Charlotte L. Wirth, District Judge

18th District Court - Wayne (D18)

36675 Ford Rd.
Westland, MI 48185
(734) 595-8720

Honorable Mark A. McConnell, Chief Judge
Honorable Sandra A. Cicirelli, District Judge

19th District Court - Wayne (D19)

16077 Michigan Ave.
Dearborn, MI 48126
(313) 943-2060

Honorable Sam A. Salamey, Chief Judge
Honorable William C. Hultgren, District Judge
Honorable Mark W. Somers, District Judge

20th District Court - Wayne (D20)

25637 Michigan Ave.
Dearborn Heights, MI 48125
(313) 277-7480

Honorable David Turfe, Chief Judge
Honorable Mark J. Plawecki, District Judge

21st District Court - Wayne (D21)
6000 N. Middlebelt Rd.
Garden City, MI 48135
(734) 793-1680

Honorable Richard L. Hammer, Jr., Chief Judge

22nd District Court - Wayne (D22)
27331 S. River Park Dr.
Inkster, MI 48141
(313) 277-8200

Honorable Sabrina L. Johnson, Chief Judge

23rd District Court - Wayne (D23)

23365 Goddard
Taylor, MI 48180
(734) 374-1334

Honorable Geno Salomone, Chief Judge
Honorable Joseph D. Slaven, District Judge

24th District Court - Wayne (D24)

6515 Roosevelt Rd.
Allen Park, MI 48101
(313) 928-0535

Honorable John T. Courtright, Chief Judge
Honorable Richard A. Page, District Judge

25th District Court - Wayne (D25)

1475 Cleophus
Lincoln Park, MI 48146
(313) 382-8603

Honorable Gregory A. Clifton, Chief Judge
Honorable David J. Zelenak, District Judge

27th District Court - Wayne (D27)

2015 Biddle Ave.
Wyandotte, MI 48192
(734) 324-4475

Honorable Randy L. Kalmbach, Chief Judge

28th District Court - Wayne (D28)

14720 Reaume Parkway
Southgate, MI 48195
(734) 258-3068

Honorable James A. Kandrevas, Chief Judge

29th District Court - Wayne (D29)

34808 Sims Ave.
Wayne, MI 48184
(734) 722-5220

Honorable Laura Redmond Mack, Chief Judge

30th District Court - Wayne (D30)

12050 Woodward Ave.
Highland Park, MI 48203
(313) 252-0300

Honorable Brigette R. Officer-Hill, Chief Judge

31st District Court - Wayne (D31)

3401 Evaline Ave.
Hamtramck, MI 48212
(313) 876-7710

Honorable Paul J. Paruk, Chief Judge

32A District Court - Wayne (D32A)

19617 Harper Ave.
Harper Woods, MI 48225
(313) 343-2590

Honorable Daniel S. Palmer, Chief Judge

33rd District Court - Wayne (D33)

19000 Van Horn
Woodhaven, MI 48183
(734) 671-0201

Honorable Jennifer Coleman Hesson, Chief Judge
Honorable James Kurt Kersten, District Judge
Honorable Michael K. McNally, District Judge

34th District Court - Wayne (D34)

11131 Wayne Rd.
Romulus, MI 48174
(734) 941-4462

Honorable Tina Brooks Green, Chief Judge
Honorable Brian A. Oakley, District Judge
Honorable David M. Parrott, District Judge

35th District Court - Wayne (D35)

660 Plymouth Rd.
Plymouth, MI 48170
(734) 459-4740

Honorable James A. Plakas, Chief Judge
Honorable Michael J. Gerou, District Judge
Honorable Ronald W. Lowe, District Judge

36th District Court - Wayne (D36)

421 Madison Ave.
Detroit, MI 48226
(313) 965-2200

Honorable Nancy McCaughan Blount, Chief Judge
Honorable Lydia Nance Adams, District Judge
Honorable Roberta C. Archer, District Judge
Honorable Izetta F. Bright, District Judge
Honorable Demetria Brue, District Judge
Honorable Esther Lynise Bryant-Weekes, District Judge
Honorable Ruth C. Carter, District Judge
Honorable Donald Coleman, District Judge
Honorable Prentis Edwards, Jr., District Judge
Honorable Wanda Evans, District Judge
Honorable Deborah Geraldine Ford, District Judge
Honorable Ruth Ann Garrett, District Judge
Honorable Ronald Giles, District Judge
Honorable Katherine Hansen, District Judge
Honorable Shannon A. Holmes, District Judge
Honorable Patricia L. Jefferson, District Judge
Honorable Alicia A. Jones-Coleman, District Judge
Honorable Kenneth J. King, District Judge
Honorable Deborah L. Langston, District Judge
Honorable Leonia J. Lloyd, District Judge
Honorable Miriam B. Martin-Clark, District Judge
Honorable William McConico, District Judge
Honorable Donna R. Milhouse, District Judge
Honorable B. Pennie Millender, District Judge
Honorable Cylenthia LaToye Miller, District Judge
Honorable David Perkins, District Judge
Honorable Kevin F. Robbins, District Judge
Honorable David S. Robinson, Jr., District Judge
Honorable Michael E. Wagner, District Judge

Grosse Pte. Municipal Court - Wayne (MGP)

17147 Maumee
Grosse Pointe, MI 48230
(313) 343-5262

Honorable Russell F. Ethridge, Chief Judge

Grosse Pte. Farms Municipal Court - Wayne (MGPF)

90 Kerby Rd.
Grosse Pte. Farms, MI 48236
(313) 885-2104

Honorable Matthew R. Rumora, Chief Judge

Grosse Pte. Farms Municipal Court - Grosse Pte. Shores

Grosse Pte. Shores Division
795 Lakeshore Dr.
Grosse Pte. Shores, MI 48236
(313) 881-5503

Honorable Matthew R. Rumora, Chief Judge

Grosse Pte. Park Municipal Court - Wayne (MGPP)

15115 E. Jefferson Ave.
Grosse Pte. Park, MI 48230
(313) 822-3535

Honorable Carl F. Jarboe, Chief Judge

Grosse Pte. Woods Municipal Court - Grosse Pointe Woods - Wayne (MGPW)

20025 Mack Plaza Drive
Grosse Pte. Woods, MI 48236
(313) 343-2455

Honorable Theodore A. Metry, Chief Judge

Oakland County

43rd District Court-Hazel Park - Oakland (D43~1)

43 E. Nine Mile Rd.
Hazel Park, MI 48030
(248) 547-3034

Honorable Joseph Longo, Chief Judge
Honorable Charles G. Goedert, District Judge
Honorable Keith P. Hunt, District Judge

43rd District Court-Ferndale - Oakland (D43~2)

305 E. Nine Mile Rd.
Ferndale, MI 48220
(248) 547-8700

Honorable Joseph Longo, Chief Judge
Honorable Charles G. Goedert, District Judge
Honorable Keith P. Hunt, District Judge

43rd District Court-Madison Heights - Oakland (D43~3)

200 W. Thirteen Mile Rd.
Madison Heights, MI 48071
(248) 583-1800

Honorable Joseph Longo, Chief Judge
Honorable Charles G. Goedert, District Judge
Honorable Keith P. Hunt, District Judge

44th District Court - Royal Oak - Oakland (D44)

PO Box 20
400 E. 11 Mile Road
Royal Oak, MI 48068
(248) 246-3600

Honorable Derek W. Meinecke, Chief Judge

Honorable James L. Wittenberg, District Judge

45th District Court - Oakland (D45)

13600 Oak Park Blvd.
Oak Park, MI 48237
(248) 691-7433

Honorable Michelle Friedman Appel, Chief Judge
Honorable David M. Gubow, District Judge

46th District Court - Oakland (D46)

PO Box 2055
26000 Evergreen Rd.
Southfield, MI 48076
(248) 796-5800

Ms. Cynthia Arvant, District Judge
Honorable Shelia R. Johnson, District Judge
Honorable Debra Nance, District Judge

47th District Court - Oakland (D47)

31605 W. Eleven Mile Road
Farmington Hills, MI 48336
(248) 871-2900
Honorable Marla E. Parker, Chief Judge
Honorable James Brady, District Judge

48th District Court - Oakland (D48)

PO Box 3200
4280 Telegraph Rd.
Bloomfield Hills, MI 48302
(248) 647-1141

Honorable Kimberly Small, Chief Judge
Honorable Marc Barron, District Judge
Honorable Diane D'Agostini, District Judge

50th District Court - Oakland (D50)

70 N. Saginaw
Pontiac, MI 48342
(248) 758-3800

Honorable Cynthia Thomas Walker, Chief Judge
Honorable Ronda Fowlkes Gross, District Judge
Honorable Michael C. Martinez, District Judge
Honorable Preston G. Thomas, District Judge

51st District Court - Oakland (D51)

5100 Civic Center Drive
Waterford, MI 48329
(248) 674-4655

Honorable Richard D. Kuhn, Jr., Chief Judge
Honorable Jodi R. Debbrecht Switalski, District Judge

52nd District Court - Novi - Oakland (D52-1)
48150 Grand River Ave.
Novi, MI 48374
(248) 305-6080

Honorable Robert Bondy, District Judge
Honorable Thomas David Law, District Judge
Honorable Travis Reeds, District Judge

52nd District Court - Clarkston - Oakland (D52-2)

5850 Lorac
Clarkston, MI 48346
(248) 625-4888

Honorable Joseph G. Fabrizio, District Judge
Honorable Kelley Renae Kostin, District Judge

52nd District Court - Rochester Hills - Oakland (D52-3)

700 Barclay Circle

Rochester Hills, MI 48307
(248) 853-5553

Honorable Julie A. Nicholson, Chief Judge
Honorable Lisa L. Asadoorian, District Judge
Honorable Nancy Tolwin Carniak, District Judge

52nd District Court - Troy - Oakland (D52-4)

520 W. Big Beaver Road
Troy, MI 48084
(248) 528-0400

Honorable Julie A. Nicholson, Chief Judge
Honorable Kirsten Nielsen Hartig, District Judge
Honorable Maureen M. McGinnis, District Judge

Made in United States
Orlando, FL
05 November 2026

90229832R10031